The Wright Brothers
Heroes of Flight

Carin T. Ford

Enslow Publishers, Inc.

40 Industrial Road	PO Box 38
Box 398	Aldershot
Berkeley Heights, NJ 07922	Hants GU12 6BP
USA	UK

http://www.enslow.com

Library of Congress Cataloging-in-Publication Data

Ford, Carin T.
   The Wright brothers : heroes of flight / Carin T. Ford.
      p. cm. — (Famous inventors)
   Summary: Profiles two brothers whose childhood interest in flight led them to build a successful flying machine.
   Includes index.
   ISBN 0-7660-2002-9 (hardcover)
   1. Wright, Orville, 1871–1948—Juvenile literature 2. Wright, Wilbur, 1867–1912—Juvenile literature. 3. Aeronautics—United States—History—Juvenile literature. 4. Inventors—United States—Biography—Juvenile literature. 5. Aeronautics—United States—History—Juvenile literature. [1. Wright, Orville, 1871–1948. 2. Wright, Wilbur, 1867–1912. 3. Inventors. 4. Aeronautics—Biography.] I. Title. II. Series.
   TL540.W7 F66   2003
   629.13'0092'73—dc21

                                                                        2002009197

APR 1 5 2004

CEN T

To Our Readers: We have done our best to make sure all Internet Addresses in this book were active and appropriate when we went to press. However, the author and the publisher have no control over and assume no liability for the material available on those Internet sites or on other Web sites they may link to. Any comments or suggestions can be sent by e-mail to comments@enslow.com or to the address on the back cover.

Every effort has been made to locate all copyright holders of material used in this book. If any errors or omissions have occurred, corrections will be made in future editions of this book.

Illustration Credits: Courtesy of Special Collections and Archives, Wright State University, pp. 3, 4 (R), 6 (T), 8 (L), 8 (R), 10, 11, 14, 27, 28; Library of Congress, pp. 4 (L), 6 (B), 7, 15, 17, 18, 19, 20, 21, 22, 24, 25, 26; Painet, Inc., p. 13; Wright Brothers Aeroplane Company, pp. 1, 2.

Cover Credits: Wright Brothers Aeroplane Company; Wright State University

Table of Contents

Orville, left, and Wilbur Wright

Chapter 1

Dreams of Flying

oung Orville Wright sat at his desk in school. He was seven years old. Orville and his older brother Wilbur were good students, but there was one big difference. Wilbur behaved in class, and Orville often got into trouble.

That day, Orville was not paying attention. Instead, he was playing with two pieces of wood. The teacher was angry and asked Orville what he was doing.

Sometimes Orville, above, could be a troublemaker in school. Wilbur, below, always loved to read.

Orville said he was making a machine that would fly. Someday he planned to make one big enough to carry himself and his brother.

Many years later, that is exactly what Orville and Wilbur would do. The Wright brothers would be remembered throughout history. They became the first people to build an airplane with an engine and controls that could really fly.

The boys were the youngest sons of Milton and Susan Wright. They had two older brothers and a younger sister. Wilbur was born on April 16, 1867, in Indiana. Orville was born on August 19, 1871, in Ohio.

Milton Wright worked as a church

bishop. In his job, he traveled to churches in many towns. He liked to bring presents home to his children.

One day, Mr. Wright brought home a toy helicopter. A rubber band made it fly. Wilbur, eleven, and Orville, seven, loved the helicopter. The boys built more helicopters just like the toy their father had given them.

Their home had two libraries—one upstairs and one downstairs. All the Wright children began

The Wrights lived in this house in Dayton, Ohio, for more than forty years.

reading when they were very young. Mr. and Mrs. Wright wanted them to be curious about the world. And they were—especially Wilbur and Orville.

Milton Wright worked for the church. Susan Wright was very handy with tools.

The brothers were as close as twins. Yet they were very different. Orville was shy but always eager to come up with new inventions. Wilbur was more friendly, and he liked to read much of the time.

There was a special bond between the brothers that lasted all their lives. Sometimes they would find themselves whistling the same song at the same moment. Wilbur said that he and Orville "lived together, played together, worked together, and in fact thought together."

Chapter 2

School and Work

The Wright brothers had their own ways of doing things. Orville became Dayton, Ohio's top math student—although his teacher still had to keep an eye on him to make sure he behaved.

Wilbur was once told that his answer to a math problem was wrong. The teacher asked a girl in the class to help him. After a short while, Wilbur convinced both the girl and the teacher that *his* answer was right.

Orville in his 1890 high school picture.

Neither boy graduated from high school. Orville became interested in the printing business. Even as a teenager, Orville had his own print shop and published a newspaper.

Wilbur hoped to go to college and become a teacher. But when he was almost eighteen, he had an accident while ice-skating. His mouth and face were hurt. This was the start of a difficult time for Wilbur.

He began to have heart problems, too. For the next few years, Wilbur rarely left home and was very gloomy. He spent his days reading and caring for his mother, who was sick. She died in 1889.

As Wilbur began to get better, he joined Orville in the printing business. Together, the brothers built their own printing press. They made it out of an old gravestone and pieces of wood and metal.

Wilbur also wrote articles for the newspaper. Before long, Wilbur was listed as the editor, and Orville was the publisher. The brothers were now real partners. For the first time, they began calling themselves "the Wright Brothers."

The newspaper did not make very much money. So the brothers looked for another business to get involved in. They decided to open a bicycle shop.

As young men, Orville and Wilbur printed this weekly newspaper.

Chapter 3

From Bicycles to Planes

rville and Wilbur were in their early twenties when bicycles became very popular. Everyone wanted one.

Only a few years earlier, the bicycle had been a machine with a huge front wheel and a tiny rear wheel. It was hard to ride, costly, and dangerous. By the late 1800s, bicycles had two smaller wheels, both the same size. They were safer and easier to ride.

The Wright brothers became interested in bicycles as a sport and as a business. Orville liked to ride in races. The brothers built, fixed, and sold bicycles, too. The Wright Cycle Company was a big success.

Orville also enjoyed working on other kinds of inventions. He made a calculator to multiply numbers. He created a typewriter that was easier for people to use.

This style of early bicycle was called a high-wheeler.

The Wright brothers built bicycles in their shop.

The brothers were happy with their work. Then something else caught their attention—flying.

Other inventors were making glider planes. These aircraft had no engines. They used the wind for power. The Wright brothers were excited to think about building their own flying machine.

The brothers believed that for a flying machine to stay up in the air for a long time, it would need an engine. They also thought the pilot had to be able to control the way the aircraft turned and flew in the air.

The Wright Brothers built this bicycle in 1897.

The brothers had built many bicycles. They

understood how a bike stayed up without falling over. Maybe a pilot could balance an airplane in the same way.

Wilbur and Orville read all the books and articles on flying that they could find. They had many ideas, but they were also worried. Trying to fly was very dangerous. Many people had been hurt or killed.

The brothers knew that other men had tried to build planes that could stay in the air and land safely. But one by one they had failed.

Why should the Wright brothers' luck be any different?

Orville was always trying to invent new things.

Chapter 4

Ready to Fly

The brothers began to watch birds fly. They noticed that birds tip or twist their wings in the air. That is how they keep their balance. Could the same thing be done with the wings of an aircraft?

They tested this idea by building a kite that had a pair of wings. They attached ropes to the wing tips. To balance the kite, Wilbur and Orville pulled on the ropes. This twisted the wings. It worked! The brothers could make the kite go up and down. They could roll it to the right and left. Would this work with an aircraft that was carrying a person?

In 1900, the brothers built a glider plane. To test it, they needed a place with strong winds to lift the plane into the air. They chose Kitty Hawk, North Carolina, a beach town. It had strong winds, lots of open space, and soft sands in case the plane crashed.

The brothers put the parts of the glider together in Kitty Hawk. Living in tents on the beach, the Wrights tried to fly their plane.

In 1900, the Wrights flew this glider on a string, like a kite.

There were many problems. The gusty winds often forced the glider to crash into the sands. Wilbur and Orville spent much of their time fixing broken parts.

After six weeks, the brothers headed back to Ohio. Their glider had flown, but there was still a lot more work that needed to be done.

This Wright brothers' glider was destroyed by strong winds.

Wilbur, in the glider, gets help taking off
at Kitty Hawk in 1901.

For the next three years, the brothers experimented with different wing shapes to make their planes fly farther. Each year, they went back to Kitty Hawk to test their new planes.

By 1902, Wilbur and Orville said they were done with gliders. They wanted to try a powered machine.

Now they faced a new problem. An engine with enough power for an airplane was very big and heavy.

Here, Wilbur is working in the shop of the
Wright Cycle Company.

The Wright brothers would have to build their own engine in the back room of their bicycle shop.

In the fall of 1903, they traveled again to Kitty Hawk. Their airplane looked liked two large wings with an engine on the bottom. It was called *Flyer*.

A long wooden track was laid down on Kill Devil Hill. This would give the plane a smooth surface for takeoff. Then Wilbur and Orville flipped a coin to see who would be the pilot. Wilbur won.

Flyer rolled down the track. But almost as soon as it lifted into the air, the engine stalled. The plane crashed into the sand.

The brothers spent a few days fixing *Flyer* before trying again. This time it was Orville's turn. The date was December 17, 1903.

Dressed in suits and ties, Wilbur and Orville shook hands.

The Wright brothers' 1903 airplane engine.

At 10:35 A.M., Orville got into the plane and took off down the ramp. Wilbur ran along the side, holding a wing to keep it steady.

The flight was short. It lasted only 12 seconds, and the plane traveled 120 feet. But it was enough. Orville Wright had become the first man in history to fly in a machine that was heavier than air, powered by an engine, and controlled by the pilot.

Flyer lifted into the air. Orville was lying on the wing, controlling the plane. Wilbur ran alongside.

Chapter 5

Success!

The brothers made three more flights that day, taking turns as pilot. During the last flight, Wilbur traveled 852 feet and stayed up in the air for 59 seconds—almost a whole minute!

The brothers sent a telegraph message to let their father in Ohio know what they had done. The first word in the message was "Success."

Newspaper reporters did not think the story was

THE WESTERN UNION TELEGRAPH COMPANY.
INCORPORATED
23,000 OFFICES IN AMERICA. CABLE SERVICE TO ALL THE WORLD.

This Company TRANSMITS and DELIVERS messages only on conditions limiting its liability, which have been assented to by the sender of the following message.
Errors can be guarded against only by repeating a message back to the sending station for comparison, and the Company will not hold itself liable for errors or delays
in transmission or delivery of Unrepeated Messages, beyond the amount of tolls paid thereon, nor in any case where the claim is not presented in writing within sixty days
after the message is filed with the Company for transmission.
This is an UNREPEATED MESSAGE. ROBERT C. CLOWRY, President and General Manager.

170

RECEIVED at

176 C KA CS 33 Paid.   Via Norfolk Va

Kitty Hawk N C Dec 17

Bishop M Wright

           7 Hawthorne St

Success four flights thursday morning all against twenty one mile
wind started from Level with engine power alone average speed
through air thirty one miles longest 57 seconds inform Press
home ~~Sk444~~ Christmas .
                                Orevelle Wright   525P

Orville sent this note to his father after the first successful flight.

important. Most people were not interested in flying machines.

Their flight was not big news, but that did not stop Orville and Wilbur. *Flyer* stayed in the air for only a minute, but it would change the world. The Wright brothers had proved that humans could fly.

That did not mean their work was finished. *Flyer* was hard to control, and it needed more power. The brothers spent the next two years experimenting with different engines, propellers, and controls. They made many flights at a field near Dayton. By 1905, they were able to stay in the air for more than a half hour.

A few years later, the Wright brothers sold an

airplane to the U.S. Army. This aircraft could stay in the air for an hour, and could hold both a pilot and a passenger. It was able to fly at forty miles per hour.

The brothers formed a company in 1909. The Wright Company built airplanes at its factory in Dayton and also ran a flying school.

Airplanes at that time were unstable and

Orville broke his leg in a crash in 1908.
The other man in the plane died.

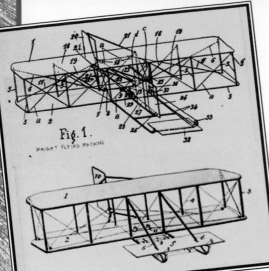

Fig. 1.
WRIGHT FLYING MACHINE

The Wright brothers drew plans for the airplanes made in their factory.

dangerous. But many people now agreed that they were the transportation of the future.

On May 30, 1912, Wilbur died of typhoid fever, a serious disease. He was forty-five years old.

Orville sold the Wright Company four years later. He kept experimenting with airplanes. He also built a laboratory and helped develop a new plumbing system, some children's toys, and a toaster.

Orville had become very famous. Yet he was as shy as he had been as a child. He was still happiest at home with his family or in his lab.

Orville died on January 30, 1948, after suffering a heart attack. He was seventy-seven years old. He had lived to see planes grow from rickety gliders of wood and fabric to high-speed metal jets carrying people and cargo all over the world.

Wilbur and Orville were two bicycle mechanics. They had been interested in flying since they were boys. Although most people said flying was impossible, the Wright brothers never gave up. They had always believed that one day people would fly.

Times were changing: This 1909 Wright brothers plane flew over some horse-drawn carriages.

With hard work and imagination, Orville and Wilbur Wright made their dream come true.

Timeline

1867~Wilbur is born April 16 in Millville, Indiana.

1871~Orville is born August 19 in Dayton, Ohio.

1889~The brothers start a printing business.

1892~The brothers form the Wright Cycle Company.

1900~Wilbur and Orville travel to Kitty Hawk, North Carolina, to test their first glider.

1903~Orville becomes the first man to fly a controlled, powered, heavier-than-air airplane.

1909~The brothers form their own airplane company.

1912~Wilbur dies on May 30.

1948~Orville dies on January 30.

Words to Know

glider plane—An aircraft that uses the wind for power. It has no engine.

laboratory—A place used for experiments and the study of science.

printing press—A machine that makes printed copies.

propeller—A device with blades that are powered by an engine to spin. The propeller pushes or pulls a plane through the air.

telegraph—A device for sending messages from one place to another over wires.

typewriter—A machine with a keyboard that prints letters and numbers onto paper.

Learn More

Books

Krensky, Stephen. *Taking Flight: The Story of the Wright Brothers*. New York: Simon & Schuster, 2000.

Schaefer, Lola M. *The Wright Brothers*. Mankato, Minnesota: Capstone Press, 2000.

Old, Wendie C. *To Fly: The Story of the Wright Brothers*. New York: Clarion Books, 2002.

Internet Addresses

The Wright Brothers Home and Cycle Shop
<http://www.hfmgv.org/exhibits/wright/default.asp>

The Wright Brothers Web Resources for Students
<http://www.stemnet.nf.ca/CITE/wright.htm>

The Wright Brothers Collection
<http://www.libraries.wright.edu/special/wright_brothers>

Index